Somebody please love me

by
Al Palmquist and Frank Reynolds
Foreword by Don Wilkerson

DIMENSION BOOKS

Bethany Fellowship, Inc.

Minneapolis, Minnesota

Dimension Books
are published by
Bethany Fellowship, Inc.
6820 Auto Club Road
Minneapolis, Minnesota 55438

Printed in the United States of America

Foreword

The authors have compiled some valuable, vital material all readers will find helpful—especially parents. The material is concise, thorough, and contains a no-nonsense approach to the problem of drug abuse—especially marijuana.

The writers are not just researchers—they have dealt with not only street addicts and users but high schoolers. They have confronted thousands in school assemblies, classes and PTA. Their material is written with a background of knowing what does and does not need to be known about drugs.

I highly recommend S O M E B O D Y, PLEASE LOVE ME.

Don Wilkerson

Preface

Lonely voices, from all walks of life, echo Tim's cry: "Somebody, please love me!" Parents, do you hear it? Do you want to hear it? You can help stem the tide of drug addiction. This book was designed with that in mind. Listen with your heart as well as your head.

1. Listen to what your kids are saying about you. Each one of the chapters in this book was written by your kids.

2. Listen to what we have to say about drug education. Drug education will help you as a parent to understand what your kids are facing.

Proper drug education is one phase in licking the drug problem. In this book we simply want you to do two things: learn about drugs and listen to what your kids are saying about you.

Acknowledgments

The authors wish to express their thanks to Paul Ingram, Andi Busti, George Abich, Jose Pacheco and Al Morganti. These five fellows have a combined total of nearly 60 years of drug addiction. Without their guidance this book could never have been written.

We also wish to thank Delcie Stewart and Michele Stoudt for taking a rough manuscript and getting it into readable form.

Contents

Chapter 1

An Open Letter to a Parent From An Addict Offspring

I am a drug user and I need help. Don't allow me to lie to you. By accepting my lies for truth, you encourage me to lie. The truth may be painful, but accept it.

Don't allow me to outsmart you. This only teaches me to avoid responsibility and at the same time lose respect for you. Don't lecture me, scold, argue with me or moralize when I am high.

Don't accept promises. This is just my method of postponing pain. Don't keep switching agreements. If an agreement is made . . . stick to it. Don't lose your temper with me. To do so will destroy you and any possibility of helping me.

Don't allow your anxiety for me to compel you to do what I must do for myself. Don't cover up the consequences of my abuse of drugs. This may reduce the immediate crisis but perpetuate the illness.

Above all, don't run away from reality as I do. Drug abuse, my illness, gets worse as my use continues. I need help from a doctor, a counsellor, a psychologist, a recovered addict . . . from God! I cannot make it alone.

I hate myself but I love the thought of being what I once was—drug free. For you to do nothing is the worst choice you can make for me. My drugged mind would welcome apathy from you. It would welcome any form of coddling, any expression of sympathy.

When my drug-free mind has a chance to function, I know that someone must be firm with me—even to the point of seeming cruel. Until you, too, can feel this way, I will remain a drug abuser . . . and who knows what else?

Never forget that misery loves company. As someone helped me to start using drugs, I, too, will help others. Don't let me compound this misery.

If you love me as a parent—or if you have only compassion for me as another human being desperately in need of help you are in a position to give—please help me to help myself.

Chapter 2

The Parent Who Is Unconcerned

Many parents are full of questions and have a genuine desire to learn about drugs. Some want to be involved, while others are too preoccupied to be concerned. For our consideration, we have divided all parents into three groups: (1) The parent who is unconcerned, (2) the parent who wants education, (3) the parent who wants to get involved.

The first group, the unconcerned parents, I am afraid, may be the biggest group. We will consider them first.

There may be many reasons for you not to be concerned. (1) You may think your child would never get involved with drugs or the people that run around in the drug culture. (2) You may think that only kids with long hair and bell-bottom pants get involved with drugs. Your child does not have long hair or wear bell-bottom pants. (3) You may think that you live in a city that is free from drugs.

From our travels we have learned quite a bit about each reason. If you think that your child would never get involved with drugs, you may be right; but you may also be wrong, and "an ounce of prevention is well worth a pound of cure." Your child may be good and still get involved. It is not only the "bad apple" that tries drugs. There are many reasons why your child might take drugs: (1) curiosity, (2) lack of education, (3) peer group pressure, (4) desire to get high, (5) an empty life, (6) an attempt to gain insight, or (7) just for kicks. Any one of these could come from a good child. I don't think any parent should think his children are exempt from drugs.

You may feel that your children wear proper clothes, and only long-hairs get high. Well, you are wrong. I know many bald-headed people who get high. I know many people who get high who have never owned bell-bottom pants. As a matter of fact, when many kids start taking drugs, they cut their hair and wear straight clothes, because they know that most parents and policemen look for certain dress and hair styles when they search for drug users.

But you still have one argument left: you live in a town or city that is drug free. We have one thing to say to you—take your head out of the sand. We have been giving drug talks and working with drug users long enough to *know* that no town is drug free. We have been in too many out-of-the-way places to believe that any town is free. Drugs are here. Let's wake up and fight it.

The general feeling in this group is any-one that takes any kind of drugs, other than alcohol of course, is a junkie and a complete social misfit. This is quite wrong. Hear what happened to one promising fellow.

George, who went through the Teen Challenge Program, was a drug addict for seven years before his parents found out. George and his dad used to watch TV together, and when a drug announcement would come on, they would both agree that it was awful to take drugs. At the time they were talking George was not only high, but he was high on heroin and had been hooked for seven years. His father was unconcerned. He had a good family. Two of his daughters were doctors, one son a lawyer, another son an engineer, and George was in college. Drugs were no part of his family. Oh, how wrong he and hundreds of parents are! Yes, it is time to wake up and be on guard.

Chapter 3
The Parent Who Wants Education

It is great to know that millions of parents want to know what is happening on the drug scene, what drugs are being used. In this chapter we are going to consider the second group, the parent who wants education. We will answer questions most asked by these parents; such as, what drugs are being used by young people? where do they get the drugs? how much do they cost? what are the effects?, etc.

There are three types of drugs that our kids are playing with: heroin, hallucinogens, and marijuana, besides alcohol. There are also two basic types of pills the kids are taking: amphetamines and sedatives (nicknamed uppers and downers).

AMPHETAMINES AND SEDATIVES

What are amphetamines and sedatives? Amphetamines are stimulants which affect the central nervous system. First produced in the 1920's, the most commonly used stimulants are benzedrine, dexedrine, and methedrine. These stimulants are also known as pep pills, ups, and speed. Other stimulants are cocaine, codeine, and methamphetamines. Methamphetamine is closely related to the amphetamines. It has similar but more potent effects.

Sedatives belong to a family of drugs which relax the central nervous system. They are known as barbiturates. Nembutal, seconal, luminal, busitol, and amytal are some popular barbiturates. They are sometimes called "goofers" and "goof balls."

What are its medical uses? Amphetamines are used to combat fatigue, relieve depression, reduce the appetite. They were first used to control colds since they shrink nasal membranes. Lately, however, new and more effective non-stimulant drugs are used to combat colds. They are also used as mood elevators and for narcolepsy. They produce a sensation of wakefulness and energetic feeling.

Codeine, an opium derivative, is used in cough medicines. It is a minor pain killer that produces slight feeling of euphoria.

Cocaine, derived from the leaves of the coca bush, is used as an anesthetic. It is legally, but not chemically, classified as a narcotic. It produces the feeling of exhilaration and is said to relieve hunger and fatigue.

Sedatives are used in many capacities. They are prescribed to induce sleep or provide a calming effect. They treat nervous conditions, mental disorders, high blood pressure, epilepsy, insomnia, and occasionally are used as a surgical aid. Morphine is an opium derivative used as a sedative and a pain killer. It produces a feeling of calmness.

What are their effects? Amphetamines cause an increase of the heart rate, raise the blood pressure, dilate the pupils, and can also cause sweating, headaches and diarrhea. When properly used they depress the appetite, check fatigue, and produce feelings of self-confidence and alertness. Excessive doses can cause high blood pressure, irregular heart rhythms, and even heart attacks. Heavy doses cause the user to become irritable and jittery. They also cause the emotions to become dulled and speech to become unclear. The user tends to become withdrawn, and when the drug wears off, he can become very depressed. An overdose of cocaine can cause paranoid activity, convulsions, and death. It is psychologically but not physically addicting. The degree and risk of abuse of codeine is very minor, because extremely large doses are required. It is physically and psychologically addictive.

When taken in normal amounts sedatives slow the pulse rate, relax the nerves and skeletal muscles, and reduce the breathing rate. The effects of large doses resemble those of alcoholic drunkenness. The user staggers about, his speech becomes slurred, and his mental and emotional facilities are impaired. Eventually, he may fall into a deep sleep. Excessive dosage of morphine may cause coma or death due to respiratory failure. Morphine is physically and psychologically addicting.

Are amphetamines and sedatives misused? There are enough amphetamines produced each year in this country to provide every person with twenty-five doses each. At least half of this supply enters illegal channels. Black market stimulants are also produced in homemade laboratories. Over-the-road truck drivers are known for their use of illegal stimulants.

Although people from all walks of life are known to be abusers of stimulants, young people are now becoming the major abusers. Many students use them while cramming for exams. Many young people take stimulants and barbiturates to obtain a simultaneous "up" and "down" feeling.

Some people are now using stimulants in its strongest form. This is done by injecting liquid methedrine ("speed") into the vein. This is an especially dangerous form of use, because extended use causes the user to lose a considerable amount of weight. The teeth also deteriorate rapidly as it tends to rob normal calcium levels in the body. Serum hepatitis is also a possibility due to the use of unsanitary hypodermics. When methedrine is injected into a vein in large doses, it can cause psychosis, disintegration of personality and even death in extreme cases.

A new way of abusing stimulants has recently come into popularity among secondary school age youth. An orange or grapefruit is rolled until the liquid is loosened. The liquid is then extracted with a hypodermic syringe. Liquid stimulants and alcohol are then reinjected into the same fruit and its contents drunk through a straw.

Since sedatives are commonly prescribed by doctors, many people feel they are safe to take in any strength. They slow the reactions, and because of this are a leading cause of accidents, especially when taken with alcohol whose effect they heighten.

Users have a tendency to take more sedatives than necessary. Overdose may cause death, and indeed they are a leading cause of accidental death.

In recent years sedatives have become the most popular form of suicide in this country. It requires no great amount of nerve to take a lethal dose. There is no pain and one simply falls into a deep sleep and finally the body becomes so relaxed that it stops functioning altogether.

Are these drugs addicting? Amphetamines do not produce a physical addiction; however, they produce a psychological dependence in which the user feels he needs these drugs to merely function in a normal way. It also tends to become a habit for mental and/or emotional reasons. The body develops a tolerance which requires increased doses. A user of stimulants acquires an increasingly large amount to produce the desired effect.

Amphetamines can cause a person to drive himself beyond his physical limits causing him to become exhausted.

Heavy doses can cause visual and/or auditory hallucinations and aggressive behavior. They have been known to cause a mental derangement called Toxic Psychosis. They have also been known to cause death, especially among obese persons who use diet pills.

Although it is not commonly known, sedatives are probably the most addictive drugs known. They are heavily addictive, both physically and psychologically. Literally thousands of people in this country are addicted to them. They have, perhaps, a stronger hold on the body than does heroin. Little controversy is heard about this fact since they are legal by prescription, are inexpensive, and the user has a continuous supply of them. Withdrawal from a barbiturate habit is often more painful than withdrawal from a heroin habit. The user suffers cramps, convulsions, nausea and delirium. He may vomit often, sometimes emitting blood. Occasionally withdrawal from a barbiturate habit causes sudden death. An excessive dose of sedatives can cause coma and death from respiratory failure. Because they obstruct clear thinking accidental overdoses occur frequently. Barbiturates are the leading cause of accidental death, often in combination with alcohol.

The danger of this drug cannot be overemphasized. Businessmen and housewives all over the country are indeed "hooked" on them without being aware of this fact, or of its dangers. Many times young people who take narcotics have started by using barbiturates and stimulants.

What are laws concerning stimulants and barbiturates? Stimulants and barbiturates can only be legally obtained by a doctor's prescription. Druggists and their suppliers are required to keep a strict accounting of their movements because of a huge illegal industry of these drugs. Illicit manufacturing and selling of these drugs bring a fine up to $10,000 and imprisonment of 1-5 years. Selling these drugs to minors brings 10-15 years and a fine of $15,000 to $20,000. Possession of them can bring a fine of $1,000 to $10,000 and a 1-3 years in jail. State laws also regulate them.

There are different behavior patterns in the abuse of alcohol and hallucinogens. Let's suppose there are three people, one an abuser of alcohol, one an abuser of hallucinogens, and one an abuser of heroin. These people are walking at night to a city that has a great wall around it. The only way to get into the city is through the front main gate, but at night the gate is closed.

If the alcohol abuser came to the gate and found it locked, he would probably get very violent, kick the gate, hit it, and maybe even rap his head against it. Most alcohol abusers are quite violent, especially when they don't get their own way.

Now if the heroin abuser came to the city and found the gate closed, he would just say, "Oh well," and lie down and go to sleep.

If the hallucinogen abuser were to come to the gate, he might knock. But, when he realizes that the gate is locked, he would probably say, "Oh well. I will go *through the key hole.*"

Yes, it is a silly story, but it does show the different behaviorial patterns in each type of drug abuser.

Approximately 8 billion pills are produced annually in the Unite States (enough to supply every man, woman and child in America with forty pills each year). One half of these find their way into the illicit market. *Selling from 10¢ to $1.00 each brings a profit of nearly $500,000,000 a year on the illegal market.* The cost to society is tremendous.

HEROIN

Heroin is a narcotic and is derived from the opium poppy, as is morphine. It depresses the brain and central nervous system and acts as a sedative and pain killer. An overdose from heroin can cause coma or death from respiratory failure. It is heavily addictive. Withdrawal usually causes severe bodily reaction.

Heroin is usually grown in Turkey, where they are permitted to grow 10 kilos. This brings a profit of $167. Often additional crops are grown, and on the "black market" a farmer can get $350 for 10 kilos. This illegal cargo is then shipped to Syria or Lebanon where the 10 kilos are reduced to one kilo (2.2 pounds) of morphine base (a crude morphine) from here the morphine base is shipped to France for the next alteration process. One kilo of morphine produces one kilo of 80% heroin. Here is where the profit begins to climb. The $350 opium is now worth $3500 (1,000% mark-up).

Eventually it reaches New York. It now sells to "connections" for $18,000 a kilo. Four kilos of 20% heroin are created from the one kilo of 80% heroin by the addition of milk sugar in the U.S., and it is now sold for $70,000. The same process is followed by the "pushers" who "cut" 20% heroin four times and end up with 16 kilos of 5% heroin. This is sold to addicts for $5 a "bag." *The profit is 117,000% mark-up.*

Heroin on the East Coast runs about $5 and $10 a bag; in the Midwest and on the West Coast the price for "a fix" is $10 and $20. Figure an addict's daily habit at $75, multiply this by 4 (which is the ratio of merchandise that must be stolen), then brought to the "fence" for cash to support his or her habit. Sometimes checks are stolen from offices, homes and businesses burglarized, individual citizens robbed, or company checks forged. An addict in desperation to get the stuff will arm himself or herself with a knife or gun, threatening and in some instances taking the life of the person resisting his effort to get the necessary money to support the habit. In many instances it is necessary to "push" dope—that is, sell it to support the habit.

Now, translated into terms of actual dollars, the cost is astronomical. Conservative estimates of heroin addicts is at 100,000.

They consume over a ton of heroin. This ton, diluted, costs the addict over $300 million, which makes it 250 times as expensive as gold.

As an example of the cost to society, it has been figured that every 100 addicts who need $30 (this is a small figure) a day to buy drugs steal $3 million in goods a year. This has caused an increase in crime. In the Chicago suburbs crime is up 57%. Addiction is responsible for 50% of the crimes committed. The cost is felt by all of us in the loss of valuable keepsakes, personal injuries, and increased insurance rates. It has slowed down production in industry, and banks have had to carry deductible insurance against forgery. Since the average age of the addict ranges between 19 and 29, it means we are losing much of the potential manpower in industry. This is also the age when youth are seeking for college education, and their addiction cuts this out, thus lowering the future potential of leadership. *This is serious!*

Addicts also, through the use of the needle, will contract tetanus, hepatitis, venereal disease, malaria, endocarditis or some other major communicable disease. These must be treated in our hospitals at an added cost to the taxpayer and to industry. Addicts treated in Federal hospitals also increase the financial cost to the community. It costs $1,000,000 for each addict "cured," and unfortunately, only 1 to 1 1/2% are cured.

LSD

What is LSD? LSD is a man-made chemical, d-lysergic acid diethylamide. First synthesized in 1938, it is so powerful that a single ounce contains 300,000 doses. LSD is very cheap to obtain, so many high school kids save their lunch money to buy it. The price is approximately 25 cents for one fix.

LSD is called a hallucinogen (mind-affecting drug), in that it produces unusual mental activity in the user. It also strongly affects the physical senses. Hallucinogens are not known to be physically addicting. Other hallucinogens include mescaline, psilocybin, peyote, DMT, and DET. LSD, mescaline and psilocybin alter the consciousness and can lead to exhilaration or depression. Studies fail to support theory that they increase creativity.

Are there medical uses for LSD? LSD has been tested as a possible aid in treatment of mental and emotional disorders and for alcoholism. In some cases persons have been improved with LSD when taken under controlled conditions, although the help is not always lasting. LSD is used for bio-medical research, but its therapeutic value is limited.

How does the drug act? Just how LSD acts is not yet known. It appears to affect chemical levels of the brain and produces changes in the brain's electrical activity. LSD seems to block out some of the brain's normal screening processes, causing it to be flooded with unselected sounds and sights.

Studies with chronic LSD users seems to show that they suffer from too much stimulation of the senses, which seems to indicate why they cannot think or concentrate well on a goal.

Why do people take LSD? Some take it "to gain more personal insight, philosophical or religious experience," others just for "curiosity," or for "kicks." In various times of history, certain drugs have been used to increase wisdom and gain religious insights. Some of these drugs include opium, ether, and alcohol. Today these drugs are known not to contain any mystical properties.

What are its effects? The average dose of LSD lasts from 8-10 hours. After this initial up and down there is another 10-12 hour period of depression which is why the user will use amphitamines at the same time in order to feel depressed. LSD is taken in a sugar cube, a pill, or can be licked off the back of an envelope or a stamp. An amount no larger than a grain of salt can produce a horrifying experience. It increases the pulse, blood pressure, and dilates the pupils. It is not physically addicting as are narcotics, but it can cause psychological dependence.

Under the influence of LSD the user's senses will seem to change. Colors appear more vivid and sounds are more noticeable. When under LSD the user thinks he is able to "pick apart" the various instruments and can see in his mind the music being produced. He can also feel both happy and sad at the same time. Some users lose their normal sense of boundaries, hence they feel like they are floating. Another effect on the user is the sense of a loss of time. He can reason logically up to a point and usually remembers what happened to him after it wears off. After a person uses LSD on a regular basis for a period of time, its effects seem to change. Instead of becoming fascinated with changes of colors and music, he now professes to use the drug as a "mystical experience." Many users say that the drug gives them a feeling of a "new birth" and "religious insight." Authorities seem to feel that use of LSD impairs concentration and changes values.

Is LSD dangerous? There have been many instances where people have had to enter hospitals because of adverse reactions to LSD. The common symptoms of adverse reactings are paranoia and panic. The user becomes fearful that he cannot stop the drug's action, and he experiences a degree of terror which makes him attempt to escape from the influence of the drug. Persons have been accidently killed and in some instances have committed suicide under the influence of LSD.

LSD users have been known to have a recurrence or "flashback" sometimes several months after the drug has worn off—that is, they feel the effects of the drug for the second time. It can come on suddenly at any time with all the effects of the first experience.

LSD has been known to cause various forms of mental disorders. Reactions from this drug range from deep depression to severe mental derangement. Another hazard due to their use is the possibility of birth defects. Although no conclusive evidence has yet been found between LSD and birth defects, it has been shown that LSD does cause birth defects in some people. Scientists believe the drug causes changes in the chromosomes, and new evidence is being compiled to confirm this fact.

Young people, with their flexible minds, seem to be more likely to be affected by LSD, with its mind-altering properties. Long-time users of LSD have been so drastically changed that it is almost impossible for them to assimilate properly with society. So they withdraw from it, hence the term "dropout."

Laws concerning LSD are as follows: Anyone who produces, sells, or disposes of LSD is subject to a $1,000 to $10,000 fine and/or imprisonment of up to 5 years. Any person over 18 who sells or gives drugs to anyone under 21 is subject to a jail sentence of 10-15 years, and a fine of up to $20,000. Mere possession of LSD can bring a fine of $1,000 to $10,000 and 1-3 years in jail.

What is a "good trip" and a "bad trip"? In the parlance of the LSD user, the good trip consists of pleasant imagery and emotional feelings. The bad trip or "bummer" is the opposite. Perceived images are terrifying and the emotional state is one of dread and horror. Bad trips may lead to panic over fear of losing one's mind or paranoia (acute suspicion of others). Long-lasting mental illness has resulted from the use of hallucinogens, as has accidental suicide. Trips can recur months after taking initial dose.

What is a "flashback"? A flashback is a recurrence of some of the features of the LSD state days or months after the last dose. It can be invoked by physical or psychological stress, or by medications such as antihistamines, or by marijuana.

Those individuals who have used LSD infrequently rarely report flashbacks; intensive use seems to produce them more frequently. Often a flashback occurring without apparent cause can induce anxiety and concern that one is going mad. This can result in considerable fear and depression and has been known to culminate in suicide.

Are people more creative under or after LSD? People who have taken LSD feel more creative. Whether they actually are or not is difficult to determine. In studies done to compare individuals' creative capabilities before and after LSD experiences, it was found that no significant changes had occurred. Creativity might conceivably be enhanced in a few instances, but it is diminished in others because LSD may reduce the motivation to work and execute creative ideas.

Do you really get to know yourself after taking LSD? The *illusion* that one obtains insights about one's personality and behavior while under LSD may occur. From an analysis of these "insights" and of subsequent behavior, it is doubtful that true insights happen with any regularity.

Is there much research on the use of LSD? In the past three years, more than 300 investigators have been given supplies of this drug through the National Institute of Mental Health to carry out research. Considerable important work is continuing.

What is the source of illicit LSD? Almost invariably, illicit LSD comes from clandestine laboratories or is smuggled in from abroad. The precursors, lysergic acid and lysergic acid amide, can be converted into lysergic acid diethylamide (LSD) by a proficient chemist who has a reasonably well-equipped laboratory.

When obtained from illicit sources, the quality of LSD varies. Some LSD is fairly pure; other samples contain impurities and adulterants. The amount contained in each capsule or tablet usually differs greatly from the amount claimed by the "pusher." The user has no way of knowing the quality of his LSD.

MARIJUANA

What is marijuana? Marijuana is Indian hemp (*Cannabis sativa*). The parts with the highest tetrahydrocannabinol (THC) content are the flowering tops of the plant.

The leaves have a smaller amount. The stalks and seeds have little or none. THC is believed to be the active ingredient in marijuana. Many other compounds are present in marijuana, but they do not produce the mental effects of the drug.

Does marijuana vary in strength? Yes. Some marijuana may produce no effect whatsoever. A small amount of strong marijuana may produce marked effects. The THC content of the plant determines its mind-altering activity, and this varies from none to more then 2% THC. Because THC is somewhat unstable, its content in marijuana decreases as time passes.

The plant that grows wild in the United States is low in THC content compared to cultivated marijuana, or the Mexican, Lebanese, or Indian varieties. Climate, soil conditions, the time of harvesting and other factors determine the potency.

How is marijuana used? In this country, it is generally smoked in self-rolled cigarettes called "joints." It is also smoked in ordinary pipes or water pipes. Marijuana and hashish can also be added to foods or drinks.

How long do the effects of marijuana last? This depends upon the dose and the person. A few inhalations of strong marijuana can intoxicate a person for several hours. Weak marijuana will produce minimal effects for a short period of time. When a large amount is swallowed, the effects start later but persist longer than when the same quantity is smoked.

Does the individual's tolerance to marijuana vary with repeated use? The development of tolerance to marijuana does not occur. Some people speak of "reverse tolerance." By that they mean that a person may require less marijuana in order to reach a specific "high." This is basically a matter of learning how to smoke the drug and what effects to look for.

Do heavy users suffer physical withdrawal symptoms like the narcotic addict? No. Sudden withdrawal may provide restlessness and anxiety in a few persons who daily smoke large amounts of hashish, but true withdrawal symptoms as seen in the heroin addict do not develop.

Does the heavy use of marijuana affect the personality development of the young person? It can. By making marijuana use a career, the young person avoids normal life stresses and the problems that are an intrinsic part of growing up. He therefore misses the opportunity to mature to his full physical and mental potential. In addition, the developing personality is known to be susceptible to the effects of all mind-altering substances.

How does marijuana get onto the Black Market? Although truckload lots are sometimes detected, most marijuana smuggling and sales are small-time operations of a few pounds or less. Organized criminal syndicates have not been involved to date.

A recent article on marijuana reports that considerable quantities of marijuana come from Mexico where it sells for $10 a pound raw. "Manicured" marijuana sells for $20 to $40 per pound. A "load," usually of 100 to 200 pounds, is brought into Chicago by a "mule," a person who delivers the "load." The raw marijuana is valued at $100 when it crosses the border. From each pound 1,500 "reefers" (cigarettes) are made. *Sold for $1.00 each would mean a profit of $1,400.* One report says that San Diego high school kids spend $10 to $15 a week for "pot" (marijuana). The rest of marijuana is acquired locally. Hashish is made in the Near East and is smuggled into the U.S. Young people themselves account for most acquisition and sales, according to the Bureau of Narcotics and Dangerous Drugs.

Does marijuana have any medical uses? Marijuana has no approved medical use in the U.S. Some researchers are attempting to determine whether THC may have appetite-enhancing, anticonvulsant, or antidepressant capabilities.

Lately the popularity of marijuana has increased greatly in this country. In more remote areas marijuana is grown in large areas, sometimes covering several acres in size. In urban areas young people are growing it in backyard gardens and in flower pots under the guise of something else. The plant is very handy and requires very little care for successful growth.

Marijuana has been used by man for some 5,000 years. It was first used in China and in India as a pain killer to aid in surgery.

Today it has no medical use, since advances in medicine have produced far more effective surgical aids. Its only use now is solely for its intoxicating effect.

How widely is it used? In the last decade or so the use of marijuana has multiplied many times, especially among the young people. Where once its use was restricted mainly to a small number of adults, we now find it being used almost exclusively by teenagers and even as young as children of elementary school level. A considerable amount is used in the social set.

Marijuana is legally, but not chemically, classified as a narcotic. Reactions to the use of marijuana range from excitement to depression. Sense of time and distance become distorted. It is dangerous if the user is driving a car, as with a driver who is under the influence of alcohol, because his depth perception becomes distorted.

Under marijuana's influence a person is likely to become hungry, especially for sweets. It also tends to dehydrate the body. In the early stages the person may appear animated and hysterical with rapid, loud talking and bursts of laughter. In the late stages the person is sleepy or stuporous.

When a person first starts using the drug, he often gets giggly and acts childlike. Life seems brighter, he feels more aware, and music sounds better. After a period of use the user may feel that his consciousness has become more introspective and contemplative. Over an extended period of use many users become quiet and shy. They find it difficult to communicate with others and in general become anti-social.

How does marijuana affect judgment? A user of marijuana can become accident-prone because his sense of reality is distorted. Under its influence a person tends to have difficulty in making decisions that require clear thinking. He may be easily swayed by other people's decisions. In general, it affects tasks that require good reflexes and thinking.

What are the laws dealing with marijuana? Under federal law, possession of marijuana is punishable by 2-10 years imprisonment for the first offense, 5-20 years for further offenses. In each of these offenses a fine of up to $10,000 is applicable also. A person 18 years or older is subject to these laws. Recently these laws have been in a process of change. State laws may vary according to the state where the offense was committed.

What are the risks which involve young users? Besides the many legal complications which affect young users of marijuana there are other, more severe risks that can affect the psychic and the emotions. Although no definite statements can be made, it is safe to say that extended use of marijuana does produce a personality change. A harmful effect on personality growth and development of the young is suspected but not proven. This change may not be brought about entirely by the drug itself but is due partly by the environment in which the marijuana user exists. Young users seem to exist in two different worlds. One is the non-users or "straight" world, as at home, at school, or at work. The other is the social life of the user, whereby he almost invariably will associate with other users. Severe emotional trauma can result from this type of living because many young people cannot adequately fit into either of these worlds.

Is marijuana addictive? Although marijuana is not addictive in a physical sense whereby the body develops a need for the drug, in many instances it does produce a psychological addiction. Long-time effects are not known. Authorities call this a dependence rather than an addiction since it is of the mind rather than of the body. Nevertheless, this dependence can cause emotional and psychological trauma.

Does marijuana lead to narcotics? Although marijuana itself does not lead to narcotics, it is true that a person who uses marijuana would be likely to use other drugs also. Another factor is that in the circles where a person obtains marijuana, he is also likely to have access to stronger drugs. A recent survey showed that 80% of the narcotics addicts in large cities had started by using marijuana.

Let's hear how Jim got involved with hard drugs:

Every drug user I have ever met, myself included, was first turned on by his best friends. My particular group of friends were the upper middle class: professional men's kids, maids, Cadilacs, country clubs, the Jet Set scene.

One night my friends surprised me by pulling out some joints of marijuana. It wasn't long before the joint came to me, but I passed it on without smoking it. Minutes later my friends were different. They began to laugh and go through new, unusual actions. The next night the same thing happened; but I wasn't about to be their 'freak attraction,' so, I joined in with the group.

I dropped far from the violence of reality—the war, police, the establishment. All became a "bla." I enjoyed marijuana so much that I continued smoking for a month, noon and night. Then one day a "dry spell" came (no grass in the area). I wanted to get high, so I went home and took a bottle of my dad's sleeping pills. I brought them to one of my friend's, who was a doctor's kid and had some knowledge of certain pills. We concluded that one could get high on them and we did. It was a different kind of high than the grass, but it was groovy.

Days passed until all of the pills were taken, and there was still no grass around. Since I was in a drug environment, I met heads using other drugs. One sauce head told us about the beautiful high from a certain cough syrup. Unable to get any pills or grass, and merely wanting to groove, we went to a drugstore and bought this cough syrup. It was a good high, but we ran out of it in a few weeks.

Next, not having any of these drugs, we tried acid (LSD). I found myself looking forward to that stupor every day, and I now realized that drugs were a mental dependency. It wasn't a physical thing.

After hassling one day in an unsuccessful attempt to acquire drugs, I became very uptight, frustrated, and weary. I thought of a friend who was shooting numorphan, a pain killer used on cancer patients. I called him, and after explaining the circumstances he told me that he would turn me on for free.

This was a great high, the best of all. Daily I kept getting off with him. This kept on for over a month, and then he told me to go elsewhere to get my drugs. Up until that time everything was smooth and cool. Now, my so-called friends who turned me onto pot no longer wanted anything to do with me. The groovy times were over.

I realized I had become physically addicted. Life now was like playing Russian Roulette. I quickly learned the angles and naturally geared my thought pattern for this "new society." For the one who had just wanted to be in with his friends, life had really changed. I now turned to hustling, conning, and doing the things that an addict does to support his habit.

Time passed and I was arrested four times. On the fourth arrest I sat in the cell and thought about what drugs had done to me. I recalled acquaintances who all had been arrested for drugs, two for taking an overdose. They were now dead. Others were now in mental institutions. I was disillusioned, and the motivation and desires that I had once had vanished.

I came out of jail and tried to get on the methadone program. After an interview I was told I was not eligible for the program because I wasn't a "hard-core" junkie. Their classification for "hard core" meant five years of use or more. I thanked them and told them that I was going back and do my thing for a couple more years, and if I wasn't dead or in jail or in some nut-house, I would be back to get on their program. He then said that they had group therapy meetings for people in my condition. I had nothing to lose, so I tried it. In fact, I went for eleven months, but I was still on drugs.

I can't say these meetings didn't help. They made me a happier junkie. I met with fifteen other junkies, and we exchanged information on who had drugs and how we got them. We also got high together before and after the meetings.

However, I was still searching for a solution. So I entered two more drug programs simultaneously. Time passed and I was still on drugs.

One night at a group therapy meeting a friend of mine came to the door. He was always doing twice as many drugs as anyone else and was ten times crazier. If you have ever seen a junkie, you have probably noticed that they don't smile, but Sammy had a smile from ear to ear. His face just shone; something was different.

He told the group where he had been and what happened to him. Being high I didn't listen, but afterwards I was envious. I walked over to Sammy and said, "I don't know what you got or where you've been, but I want it too." For the first time in Sammy's life he was together, with a capital T. He explained about the ministry of Teen Challenge and how Christ had changed his life.

I came to Teen Challenge and gave Christ a chance to change my life. Not only did He take my drug desire away, but my motivation and goals have been restored. Colors have returned to colors, and people to people. Praise God, life is worth while, worth living, worth hacking. Now I have something more than a synthetic to offer.

In the past few years the marijuna subject has been one of the hottest issues in this country. There are many so-called experts who say you should smoke pot, it won't hurt you, and it definitely should be legalized.

After several years of working with drug addicts, we've come to the conclusion that those who have been on drugs are the real experts and they are the ones to whom we should listen. Almost all the people who come to Teen Challenge claim they started with marijuana, and it led them on to something else. The testimony you have just read is the story of several fellows. Jim never said that there was an element or chemical in marijuana that caused him to go on, but listen again to what he said.

He said if he didn't take marijuana he would feel like a 'freak attraction.' The people he was running with were involved in marijuana smoking. He did not want to be called a freak, so he joined in. He loved the high he got. He kept getting high for about a month. Then one day a dry spell came. There was no marijuana to be found anywhere, but he wanted to get high. He wanted to be groovy. His mental attitude was an attitude that wanted to be high. Because of this attitude he tried cough syrup, various pills, until one day somebody offered him some new morphine. After he took that he felt this high was ten times better than anything he ever got from marijuana. Somebody then told him about heroin. After one shot of heroin he felt this was the best high of all. Heroin was so good that he wouldn't think of smoking marijuana or anything else now. After a short time he got hooked.

We feel at Teen Challenge that marijuana does lead on, not necessarily to heroin addiction, but it leads to other drugs. When kids start smoking marijuana, they start hanging around with drug-oriented people. Somebody always has something that is better than marijuana. They not only hang around with drug oriented people, but their desire to be high increases. That desire alone will cause them to try any new thing offered. This chain of events can be triggered by the experimenter. Whether or not there is this psychological bent lying dormant, who can tell. There are many people that fit the description of being prone to alcoholism that never become alcoholic because they didn't start. To talk of legalizing marijuana is to open the door to a whole new "can of worms."

The argument is given: "It is no more harmful than alcohol or tobacco." This is no argument. Look at the devastation both of these *legal* drugs cause. Look at the cost to control and then the cost trying to overcome the results of these habits.

Then listen to Dr. Buckley of Pittsburgh University, who is doing original research on marijuana. "Let's not talk about legalizing something we know so little about. If we knew in 1923 what we know about tobacco smoking, it would not be on the market." We have seen the psychological effects on many. Over and over we have had fellows tell us how paranoid they felt when using marijuana heavily. For years "so-called professionals" argued against this. Now it has been observed many times.

Just because they want to get high, many, many wind up hard-core drug addicts.

Let me share with you the opening testimony of a dozen of our Teen Challenge fellows, as to what they said about marijuana.

GEORGE: "I wanted peace, love and satisfaction. I couldn't seem to get any of these things in my world, so I started searching for it. I started to rebel and drink heavily. From drinking I went to drugs—marijuana, then cocaine, bar-

41

biturates, LSD, and finally mainlining heroin. None of these things solved my problems. As a matter of fact, drugs gave me more problems."

JOHN: "At first it was just a little pot, then a few pills. But six years later, when I looked back over my drug experience, I found I had experimented with pot, hash, barbiturates, pep pills, speed, LSD, THC, mescaline, morphine, and was at present fighting a life-and-death battle to stop using heroin, a drug I had become physically and mentally dependent on."

NESTOR: "I started on my way to drugs twelve years ago, when I began to take marijuana. Then I went to pills, heroin, cocaine and speed."

JERRY: "I started playing with drugs in 1963. My best friend offered me a stick of marijuana. I took it, and it opened the way to six years of hard drugs. I, like so many addicts, said that I would never get hooked."

ERNEST: "I started smoking pot at age 11. That didn't satisfy me, so I started taking pills and drinking cough syrup. That didn't thrill me either. I was looking for something to make me happy, so at the age of 16 I got my first shot of heroin. From then on I thought I'd found happiness; however, it wasn't anything but three long years of hell on earth."

CARLOS: "I started using drugs at age 15. I began with pot and then went on to higher drugs, searching for something. In a few months I was hooked on heroin. I had a $25-a-day habit, which became very difficult to support."

EMMANUEL: "I never believed or trusted anyone. From the time I was 14 until I enlisted in the Army, my life was a round of gang fights, wine and marijuana. While with the Army I was introduced to opium."

KURT: "My first step toward drug abuse was when I was 13 years old. Marijuana was the first on the list. Things went smoothly for quite a while. I would smoke marijuana and really get excited with the strange feeling it gave me. This didn't last, though. Before I knew it I was offered different types of pills, including LSD. There was no question in my mind—I wanted to get higher, so I took whatever came my way."

DAVID: "I smoked pot for two years. It wasn't long before I was taking 'goof balls' and hanging around the streets. It was here that I started getting into trouble. These 'goof balls' had me bound for three years. I used to tell myself that I would never use heroin, but what I didn't realize was that my habit was getting bigger and the pills no longer could supply my need. I had to resort to heroin."

DAVID V.: "I spent two years in a detention home. I was released at the age of 12, and at this time I was introduced to pot. After my first joint I thought I had found heaven on earth because all I wanted to do was to get high. After a while I went to Jersey City and started shooting heroin."

VICTOR: "I started out seven years of drug addiction by using marijuana when I was 12 years old. I went on to pills and other drugs until I became a slave to heroin."

RAFAEL: "I started using drugs when I was very young. It started out like most cases—with marijuana. I then graduated to harder and 'better' things like heroin. After a while marijuana didn't give me a big kick anymore. It got to the point where all I wanted to do was get high."

FELIPE: "My life of drug abuse began at the age of 14 when I was first introduced to pot and other drugs in pill form. For three years I roamed Brooklyn, lost in a world full of lies. Having lost all interest in school by the age of 16 I dropped out, and I began to look for a way to straighten out my life again. I had lost all respect for my parents and refused all the love they had to offer me."

Who are the experts? The fellows who have lived the scene.

Chapter 4

The Parent Who Wants To Get Involved

It is one thing to want to receive information about the drug scene, but it is still another to want to get involved. This third group of parents wants to help, and getting involved is going to be one way to stem the tide of drug abuse. Before answering the many questions from this group, let me point out a very important fact: kids *do not want to be moralized.*

While walking through our dorm one day I noticed a sign on one of the doors; pictured were two hippies talking to each other. One said to his friend, "Hey, man, did you know that cleanliness is next to godliness?" The second hippie answered, "I don't know; I haven't seen either one lately." Unfortunately, there is a lot of truth to this.

At an in-service training session for school administrators, we arrived about an hour early to hear another group present its program. One of the administrators asked a question dealing with what not to tell kids. They gave a very fast reply,

"Don't moralize and don't turn them in."

What does it mean to moralize?

At a school assembly a young girl stood to her feet and said, "Last night my mother came to me and said, 'Honey, don't smoke pot; it's bad for you, and it's immoral.' " The young girl said she was not sure about the moral implications about pot, but when her mother told her about the awfulness of pot she had a cocktail in one hand and a cigarette in the other. This girl said, "I'm sick and tired of phony sermons. I am sick of people saying 'Do as I say, not as I do'!" *That is moralizing.*

If we are going to educate our children, or our friends, we had better take an honest look at ourselves. If we are depending on a chemical and abusing drugs, we are not going to educate anyone.

Kids are saying "Don't moralize me." They are correct. Let's stop moralizing and start living an example. Someone very wise said many years ago, "Actions speak louder than words." Simply said, but oh, so true.

WHAT CAN YOUR TEENAGER DO TO STOP DRUG ABUSE?

1. Get the facts about dangerous drugs so that you can respect and not abuse drugs.
2. Learn from the experiences of others what losses occur from self-administered drugs.
3. Be vocal about your not using drugs.
4. Share your knowledge of drugs with other teens.

5. Help organize other youth in your school and form a teen council to educate teens.
6. Report to proper authorities those who are pushing drugs in your area.
7. Keep your own body strong. Don't start smoking cigarettes. Do get involved in the wholesome competitive sports at school.
8. Be careful about your own associations. To keep company with a drug user only increases the chances of your own involvement.
9. Do your thing to keep the lines of communication open at home . . . confidence is a two-way street. Confidence, respect, and acceptance at home lessen the need for acceptance by the in-crowd of drug users.
10. Spiritual involvement is next on the list. Make a personal commitment to the Lord Jesus Christ, share your faith, become involved in a worthwhile youth related church program. Your personal peace and inner security will help other teens to see that drug involvement is a "bummer," and that normal, well-adjusted and healthy individuals do not need this chemical crutch to adjust to life.

HOW CAN WE RECOGNIZE HARD-CORE ADDICTION?

Let us explain addiction—Medically, in order for a drug to get the label "addictive," they mean a person using this drug will suffer physical withdrawal pains if they stop using the drug. Because a drug is not addictive does not mean it is not dangerous. Mental dependence can be as much of a problem as physical dependence. It is difficult to define the fine line between the two.

The primary thing to look for is a drastic, radical change in behavior. For instance, a person who is becoming habitually involved or hooked to drugs will have a behavior change that can easily be detected:

1. Avoiding parents, or not able to look them in the eye.
2. A pattern break in general everyday habits and procedures.
3. Radical clothes change such as sloppiness.
4. Radical attitude change, becoming very sensitive, more than their usual behaviorial attitude, and very defensive, argumentive, aggressive with fault-finding and guilt accusations.
5. Speech slur, thick tongue, dry mouth, sometimes inarticulate (pertaining to barbiturates and amphetamines).
6. Constantly sleepy, droopy eyes, head dropped in a nod (pertaining to barbiturates or heroin).
7. Decrease in appetite, extreme loss of weight (pertaining to amphetamine, speed or heroin).
8. Constantly restless, can't sleep, eyes and nose run, constantly yawning

(pertaining to sickness or withdrawal from heroin).

9. Items missing from room or house: clothing, jewelry, kitchen appliances, anything of value to be sold or exchanged for drugs.
10. Bruised marks on arms or legs, needle marks on veins.
11. Total change of associates.
12. Secretive telephone conversations.
13. Giddiness, or laughing at commonplace things.
14. Wearing of dark glasses.
15. Lying—covering for friends and activities.

However, these signs may give evidence of other changes in the person's life without any drug involvement. An adolescent or adult going through any serious traumatic psychological change may reflect the majority of these symptoms. Nonetheless, a parent, husband or wife knows the individual well enough to recognize the changes.

Whenever you feel you have undoubtable evidence of drastic attitude change, confront the individual immediately of your suspicion naming particulars as to why you feel as you do. Then notice the behavior as to whether it gives additional warrant to your accusations. However, we urge that you be fair, watchful and honest to yourself and to the person. If in doubt, wait for additional evidence: if the person is truly involved with drugs, the evidence will come.

If you are close to your children you will

be able to recognize the difference between these actions described and the normal problems of adolescence. The tragedy is that too many of us are involved in our own little world. When an arrest comes or someone outside points out the problem, we are amazed and say, "I didn't realize this was happening!"

Any radical change in attitude or behavior should be cause to be concerned. Even though it may not be involvement in drugs, there may be personal problems that need dealing with.

WHY ARE DRUGS BEING ABUSED THESE DAYS?

Drug abuse is not a new phenomenon. Varying forms of drug abuse have been present for years in the United States and other countries. There are many reasons for the current epidemic of drug misuse. Very broadly, drug abuse can be described as an effort by individuals to feel different than they do. Many drugs temporarily allow their users to evade frustrations, to lessen depression and feelings of alienation, or to escape from themselves. Such misuse of drugs, of course, does not produce any improvement in the problems of the individual or society. Rather, it is a flight from problems.

Some of the factors in the great "turn on" of recent years are:

1. The widespread belief that "medicines" can magically solve problems.

2. The numbers of young people who are dissatisfied or disillusioned, or who have lost faith in the prevailing social system.

3. The tendency of persons with psychological problems to seek easy solutions with chemicals.

4. The easy access to drugs of various sorts.

5. The development of an affluent society that can afford drugs.

6. The statements of proselytizers who proclaim the "goodness" of drugs.

DO DRUG ABUSERS TAKE MORE THAN ONE DRUG AT A TIME?

People who abuse one drug tend to take all sorts of drugs. Some of them say they are looking for a new "high." Some will take any drug to get outside themselves. Some play chemical roulette by taking everything, including unidentified pills.

WHAT SORT OF PROGRAM COULD MAKE A REAL IMPACT ON OUR DRUG ABUSE PROBLEM?

1. Society should judge adults who misuse liquor or drugs by the same standards it judges young people. A double standard produces a credibility gap.

2. Children should not be continually exposed to the idea that the stresses of daily life require chemical relief.

3. Factual information about drugs

should be stressed rather than attempts to frighten people.

4. Respect for all chemicals, especially mind-altering chemicals, should be instilled in people at an early age.

5. Efforts to detect all manufacturers and large scale traffickers of illicit drugs should increase.

6. Further research in prevention, education and treatment techniques should be carried out.

WHAT CAN ONE DO TO HELP PREVENT THE SPREAD OF DRUG ABUSE?

There are a number of things an individual can do:

1. He can set a good example by not abusing drugs himself. Since he can expect his children to model their drug-taking behavior after his, he must refrain from drinking socially accepted alcoholic beverages.

2. He can learn as many facts as possible about drugs so that he will understand the problem and be equipped to discuss it in a reasonable manner.

3. If he learns that someone is peddling drugs, he should notify the authorities. It is the responsibility of both the individual and the community to keep the dealers out.

4. He should do what he can to assist anyone wanting help for a drug problem while awaiting additional aid from a trained person or a treatment facility.

5. Most important of all, he can strive to meet the ideals of parenthood, trying to

rear his children so that they are neither deprived of affection nor spoiled. He should have a set of realistic expectations for them. He should give his children responsibilities according to their capabilities, and not overprotect them from the difficulties they will encounter. A parent should be able to talk frankly to his children, and they to him.

Pain is not all bad. We may have to suffer some in order to find a solution to the problems. Covering symptoms, either physical or mental, by taking some drug, legal or illegal, does not cure the *dis-ease.*

WHAT DOES THE HEROIN ADDICT LOOK LIKE?

He may appear normal. Some of the acute symptoms associated with heroin are sniffling, flushing, drowsiness and constipation. Very contracted pupils are typical of opiate use. Some addicts may have an unhealthy appearance because of poor food intake and personal neglect. Venereal disease among female addicts is not uncommon.

Heroin addicts appear at hospitals with blood infections, hepatitis, symptoms of overdose and, more rarely, lockjaw. Fresh needle marks and "tracks" (discoloration along the course of veins in the arms and legs) are detectable during an examination. A sample of the addict's urine will reveal heroin or quinine. Barbiturate and amphetamine abuse can also be detected by urine testing.

CAN A PERSON FUNCTION
WHILE ON NARCOTICS?

If the person is tolerant to an opiate, he can usually function satisfactorily. This assumes that he is on a constant dosage level, and that his body's reaction to the drug is minimal. It merely keeps him comfortable.

This ability to perform, stay awake and alert after being kept on a maintenance level has been demonstrated with the methadone maintenance treatment. An occasional person will be drowsy.

WHAT IS IT LIKE TO TAKE
A SHOT OF HEROIN?

Generally, there is a feeling of relaxation and of being "high." This is accompanied by an "awayness" or pleasant, dreamlike state.

As tolerance develops, the "high" is generally lost. The addict then requires heroin to avoid the withdrawal sickness. In other words, at this point he is using heroin to feel normal.

IS THERE A RELATIONSHIP
BETWEEN HEROIN AND CRIME?

Many addicts had criminal records before they became addicted. Nevertheless, a direct relationship between the addicted person and criminal activity does exist because of the need for large sums of money in order to support his habit. Shoplifting, pimping, prostitution, peddling heroin, and car theft are some of the crimes to which the addict resorts. When he is feeling symptoms of withdrawal, he may commit more violent crimes in order to obtain his drug.

Addicts who are sufficiently affluent to buy heroin will not commit criminal acts. The opiate state is one of passivity rather than aggression.

WHAT ARE THE ORGANIZED CRIME ELEMENTS THAT DEAL IN NARCOTICS AND DANGEROUS DRUGS?

Trafficking in heroin is usually undertaken by the organized criminal elements based in major metropolitan areas throughout the country. These organizations have the manpower, financial ability, and internationl connections with which to procure and successfully smuggle large quantities of heroin into the United States from France and other countries. To a lesser extent, numerous individuals and independent groups smuggle illicitly produced Mexican heroin in small quantities across the Mexican border.

WHAT ABOUT THE "BRITISH SYSTEM" OF DEALING WITH HEROIN ADDICTION?

Until recently, English heroin addicts were able to obtain heroin by prescription after registering with a physician. During the past decade, however, the number of known heroin addicts rose from a few hundred to several thousand. The number of known addicts under 20 years of age increased from one in 1960 to 1,016 in 1969. (These figures are regarded as underestimates, since many addicts do not come to official attention.)

As a result of this increase, the "system" was changed in 1968. British physicians can no longer prescribe heroin. Instead, rehabilitation centers have been established for the treatment of drug addicts. In cases where total abstinence is not possible for an addict, some heroin or methadone may be prescribed. The British system is considered a failure and has been modified to meet the increasing problem of addiction. However, it has largely prevented the involvement of organized criminal elements in heroin traffic. At present, the illicit traffic consists of addicts selling their supplies to others.

WHAT ARE SOME OF THE TYPES OF PEOPLE YOU RUN INTO WHILE DEALING WITH DRUG ADDICTS?

When you are dealing with drug addicts you must realize that there is more involved than just taking drugs. It usually costs the drug addict an average of forty thousand dollars a year for his habit. In obtaining this sort of money he must turn to some type of deviate behavior to support his habit. Many drug addicts, male and female, turn to prostitution, and after a period of time many addicts will be equally addicted to prostitution.

There are several types of prostitution. The prostitute that simply walks the street soliciting her wares is the first type. There are also company prostitutes. These are young people who seek better positions at their jobs. So, in order to get ahead, they offer their services as a prostitute. Gang prostitutes usually offer their services strictly to gang members. The call girl prostitute deals with the high class, sophisticated businessman at a very high price. Drug addict prostitutes (especially women) were drug addicts before they became prostitutes. Being a prostitute is usually the easiest way for a female to obtain money for drugs. Her first problem is that she is a drug addict.

Some men who are addicts become male prostitutes in order to support their habit. In plain English, they become homosexuals to make money. This in itself may become his major problem.

Counseling a drug addict prostitute is no easy thing, especially if she is young and just starting out. She probably will not listen. Many older prostitutes that have been addicts for several years are looking for a way out. If you can show them someone else who has made it, they may listen to you. In dealing with this type of people you must be very positive, especially about the claims of Christ. Many times prostitutes believe they can't be forgiven. It is imperative that you know the Scriptures and present them in a positive manner.

A young girl came in at the end of a meeting one night and told us that she was a prostitute and was having sexual relations with her father. She felt that she had problems that could never be forgiven. We simply took her to the Scriptures and showed her that Jesus dealt with prostitutes, saved them, and cleansed them. We told her about the woman from Samaria that had had five husbands and was living with her sixth. We asked her if she felt worse than this woman. She said that she thought she was about the same as the woman in the Bible. We told her that if Christ could forgive this woman He could forgive her. All at once she said, "Christ can forgive," and bowed her head and asked God's forgiveness. Then she looked up at us, smiling from ear to ear, and said, "It works!"

Many drug addicts get involved with drugs because of severe psychological hang-ups. Many are psychotic. A psychotic person can be very happy and cheerful on the outside. With a smile on his face he can put a knife into you.

Many drug addicts are emotionally disturbed, and you must be very careful in dealing with them. We would suggest working with ex-addicts before you get involved yourself. Many drug addicts tell you they want help, but all they really want to do is get their hands on your wallet. You must remember that drug addicts need nearly $100 every day to exist. If you look like an easy touch, they may seem very sincere when all they want to do is take you for a ride.

Do not be deceived in thinking that drug addicts are ignorant people. Most drug addicts are very alert. One drug addict said that he got so good at stealing that he could walk into an appliance store and steal a radio, walk out of the store with the radio and leave the music back on the shelf. This may seem a little way-out, but drug addicts get very good at very different types of con-games. The only way you can learn the difference between someone who is for real and one who is not is to get involved.

Everyone we know who has worked with drug addicts has been conned several times. Don't let it discourage you. Just mark it off as drug education. The only way to learn about drug addicts and their ways is to get involved with them.

Chapter 5

Is There a Real Cure?

At one of the many seminars that we have attended, the thought was inflicted that once a person gets hooked, it's all over. They said we must learn to accept this, and learn to MAINTAIN a drug addict. Let's hear twelve fellows give their answers to this question.

TOM

I was born in Palmyra, New York, in 1952. At the age of 12 I started to drink with my friend; and when drugs came in, I was ready for that. At 13 I dropped my first tab of acid. I said that I'd only do it *once*, but that led on to more and more drugs until I was "high" on something every day.

I tried to stop taking acid for four years, but every time someone offered to turn me on, I was willing. Then came the day when someone told me of the love of God. At first I rejected it, and then the Spirit of God convicted my heart. On March 29, 1969, when I was on a bad trip, the Lord saved my soul. The minister that told me of God's love took me to Teen Challenge where the

Lord has healed my mind and body. I thank the Lord every day for my new life.

DON

I was brought up in a Christian home as the son of a preacher. I loved to go to parties. My parents didn't like this because they were Christians, so I changed my mind about the Christian life.

I started hanging around with the "in" crowd so they would not call me square or corny. I liked being with the fellows—hanging around, chasing girls, and making jokes. People thought I was something because I was in the "in" crowd.

Then when I was 11, I started stealing here and there. At 12 I was pretty good at stealing. A friend introduced me to spot remover. I practiced my trade (stealing) to get spot remover. A few months later I moved on to glue, and a month and a half after that I was on cough syrup. I thought things were going great because I didn't pay—I just stole it. It made me feel good, and I thought I was the "coolest" thing going.

Then my friend Calvin said, "Here, I have a cigarette called a reefer." You smoke it something like a cigarette, but it's better than spot remover and cough syrup. So I tried it. It was wonderful. I felt as if I were flying sometimes. I was introduced to heroin when I was 12. I started sniffing it, but I didn't like it. However, I kept on because I wanted to keep up with the crowd. After a while it didn't bother me. Six months later my friend Al told me I would get more kicks if I shot it. I was scared to shoot it into my vein, so I skin popped for about three months. Then they called me chicken and said to shoot it into my vein, so I did. It was so good I did it again. I did not know that it was going to ruin two more years of my life, but it did. I tried to stop, but I couldn't. I was hooked! I was arrested on January 3, 1970, and put in jail. After three months I was sent to Teen Challenge where I found the Lord Jesus Christ as my Savior. It was a very happy feeling, better than any drug I have ever taken. My life has been wonderful ever since. Now I praise God for all He's done for me.

BILL

Since an early age, I was an incorrigible youth. I would stay away from home until I was picked up by the police, family or probation officer. I was picked up finally by the authorities and sentenced to the state reformatory. There I was introduced to pills and marijuana.

After I got out I hung around with people who used drugs. My family moved to New Jersey to get me out of the environment. Within a couple of months I found myself in trouble. I was sent to the New Jersey state reform school for an indefinite period of time. Drugs were found there and I continued to abuse them. After a year I was freed and I went home. But as soon

62

as I was home I began using drugs again—ranging from pot, to speed, to acid, to heroin. I was arrested many times for using drugs. I went to psychiatrists, social workers, and many different drug programs seeking help, but to no avail.

I heard about Teen Challenge and went to the Center for an interview. The concepts were strange and new to me. Those who talked to me presented something far different than anyone or any program had offered me. They offered me a more meaningful life through having a personal experience with Jesus Christ.

I truly praise the Lord for His abundant grace and mercy upon my life. It was only by the power of Christ that I was able to leave drugs and all of the activities that go along with drug use. Not only did Jesus Christ take away the desire for drugs, but He has filled me with an overflowing joy and peace. My life is fully surrendered and yielded to doing His will. Now I would like to go into the ministry.

GEORGE

I wanted peace, love and satisfaction. I couldn't seem to get any of these things in my world, so I started searching for it. I started to rebel and drink heavily. From drinking I went to drugs — marijuana, cocaine, barbiturates, LSD, and finally mainlining heroin. None of these solved my problems. As a matter of fact, drugs gave me more problems.

Then I started to look for a solution to

get me off drugs. I entered a methadone program and also began going to a psychiatrist. At that time my nervous system was so messed up that I was smoking five packs of cigarettes daily.

Discouraged because none of these things worked for me, I started talking to my brother's girlfriend, who is a Christian and a detective from Newark, New Jersey. She claimed the only answer was Jesus Christ! She arranged for me to go to Teen Challenge in Brooklyn, New York, and there I accepted Jesus Christ as my personal Savior.

Today I have to praise God, because He is the answer to my problems, to the peace and the love that I was looking for. Not only did God take me out of a world of drugs, but He freed me from the power of sin. I no longer have to serve Satan because I met the Lord, Jesus Christ. Praise His name for His mercy and love.

JOHN

At first it was just a little pot. Then a few pills. But six years later, when I looked back over my drug experience, I found I had experimented with pot, hash, barbiturates, pep pills, speed, LSD, THC, mescaline, morphine, and was fighting a life-and-death battle to stop using heroin, a drug on which I had become physically and mentally dependent.

I tried synthetic narcotics like methadone and other drugs, along with counseling and my own will power. They all failed.

It was at this point, when all else had failed, that I came to Teen Challenge. There I found many former drug addicts who had been off drugs for five and six years and were now helping others. They said their help for staying off drugs came from God. They had had a personal experience with Jesus Christ and found Him as their Savior.

One night I got down on my knees and prayed the only prayer I could, "God, if you are real, help me!" I meant that prayer and God meant His promise, "Behold, I stand at the door and knock. If any man hear my voice, and open the door, I will come in to him and will sup with him and he with me" (Rev. 3:20).

I cannot explain what happened after that night. I can only tell you that for the first time in many years I honestly did not want to use drugs. I still had a desire for them, but I truly wanted to overcome it. More than that, I knew I had a chance to get free—not in myself, but through God!

NESTOR

I would like to start by saying that I hope that whoever reads my testimony will receive a great blessing. I started on my way to drugs twelve years ago when I began to take marijuana. Then I went to pills, heroin, cocaine and what many young people today call speed.

I tried to kick the habit myself, but never managed to do it. Then after twelve years of suffering, I thought that I had found the answer to my suffering in the methadone program. After I lost my wife and kids I said to myself, "I'm going into the hospital." Finally, I entered the methadone program for 24 days. When I got out I was worse than the first time I went in. So I found myself back taking drugs again.

One day the truth came to me in the streets of New York. Someone spoke to me about the love and the peace that God would put in my heart if I would just give Him a chance to come into my life. I became interested in what this brother was saying, as he spoke to me about a place called Teen Challenge, a ministry of God. What really stuck in my mind were his words, "What have you got to lose?"

As I walked through the doors of Teen Challenge, I felt this peace he had talked about. I have been serving the Lord Jesus Christ for six months, and they have been the best days of my life. I am now at the Teen Challenge Training Center learning more about the Word of God. The Lord opened the doors for me to attend night school. I am praying that I may go on to Bible School.

JERRY

As I am sitting here writing this, I am thinking, "Where would I be today if it were not for God's grace and love towards me?" I would probably be in jail or six feet under the ground.

I started playing with drugs in 1963. My best friend offered me a stick of marijuana.

I took it and it opened the way to six years of hard drugs. I, like so many addicts, said that I would never get hooked.

I had fun in the beginning with the fellows and girls. I was in the "in" crowd. I was still going to school, and it looked as though everything was going fine.

About six months later I remember getting ready to go to school, and I decided that I would not get high that day. I got very sick and realized for the first time that I was trapped. From that day it was no longer a game, a kick; now it started kicking me around. I became a thief, a liar, a cheat and a hustler. I found myself in eight different programs and in jails trying to find the answer to my addiction. Everytime I would find myself back in the same old bag, and it got to the point where I wanted to take my own life. I was full of hate, jealousy and a longing which the drugs did not fill.

I was in the streets, penniless, friendless. I had lost everything just to obtain dope. I decided to go to my aunt's house and steal whatever I could.

When I got to her house, she told me that if Teen Challenge could help her son Ricky, it could help me, too. I had tried everything else, so I gave it a chance.

Let me tell you that I found more than just a program. I found Jesus. He delivered me from drug addiction and sin. The areas which I tried filling with drugs, He filled with love, peace and joy. I have new hope in my life since I am now living for Him. There is nothing better than knowing Him.

ERNEST

I started smoking pot at age 11. That didn't satisfy me, so I started taking pills and drinking cough syrup. That didn't thrill me, either. I was looking for something to make me happy, so at the age of 16 I got my first shot of heroin. From then on I thought I had found happiness. However, it wasn't anything but three long years of hell on earth.

Society rejected me, my father didn't want me, but all I wanted was to find happiness. I searched for nine years. Then one day I was lying on the couch in my room, sick. I said that was all for me because I couldn't stand being sick. I told my father that I wanted out! So, he told me that he would try to find some program for me to enter. The next day he came with a long list of programs, and I picked Teen Challenge.

When I came into the program I thought the people were crazy the way they were serving God. I got down on my knees and gave my heart to God in the Chicago Center.

CARLOS

I would like to tell you how my life was transformed by the blood of Jesus. It is wonderful to serve a true God, a God that fills one's heart with joy. My life has not always been this happy. There was a time when I was bound by drug addiction; but most of all, I was bound by sin. In other words, I was lost.

I started using drugs at the age of 15. I began with pot and then went on to higher drugs, searching for something. In a few months I was hooked on heroin. I had a $25-a-day habit which became very difficult to support. I was stealing, mugging people, doing anything that had to be done in order to get that fix. I entered program after program, trying to be cured from drug addiction. I was searching for something to fill the emptiness in my heart.

One day as I was coming out of the hospital, I saw a friend of mine, Father Francis, a priest. He knew the situation I was in, and he told me there was someone who could help me, and that was Jesus Christ. At first I didn't believe him, but he gave me the address of Teen Challenge. I said to myself, "This is my last hope. If I don't make it here, I will remain an addict for the rest of my life." I went to Teen Challenge and they accepted me. There I saw all the other ex-addicts with a peace and joy within them. I could see it on their faces, but most of all I could see they had Christ in their hearts.

One night at the altar I knelt and cried out to God. Everyone prayed for me, and it was that very night that the hand of God touched me. That night I felt His presence. That night He cleansed me from all sin and unrighteousness. He filled me with His love and cleansed me with His blood. He broke the chains of sin and I accepted Him as my personal Savior. I am no longer a drug addict. I am no longer a sinner lost in the world. I am now a child of God.

EMMANUEL (SONNY)

I was like many other young black boys in the ghetto. I never believed or trusted anyone! From the time I was 14 until I enlisted in the Army, my life was a round of gang fights, wine, and marijuana.

While with the Army in Korea I was introduced to opium. I kicked the opium habit upon my return to the States, but after being sent to Vietnam, where I worked as an Engineer Supply Specialist, I began smoking marijuana heavily.

After three years I returned to Chicago with the hope of finding a good job and getting married. I started hanging around with the fellows and was soon hooked on cough syrup with codeine. A year later I was sniffing heroin and soon I was using a needle. Finally I had to quit my job and began to steal. My habit got so bad I began to take things from home and sell them. I went to a hospital, but it did not change things. I even signed myself into jail, but that did no good. Finally my family asked me not to come home anymore. I could not be trusted in the house. I ended up with no place to live and in trouble with the state. They had me turned over to the Grand Jury for possession of heroin, and I still had the habit. I made up my mind I'd be a dope-fiend till I died. I tried to get into a couple of hospitals, but I gave up.

One day I looked down the street and saw a white man and decided to go see what he was doing. I listened to him tell a fellow about the love of Jesus Christ, and I knew this was what I needed. I entered the program at Prevention in Chicago. One week later I accepted Jesus Christ as my Savior. For the first time, my life began to have meaning. I am now at the Teen Challenge Training Center in Rehrersburg, Pennsylvania. Thank God for His Son, Jesus.

KURT

I thank God for saving me from a life of drug abuse and sin. My first step toward drug abuse was when I was 13 years old. Marijuana was the first on the list. My friends told me that no matter what I was missing in life this would satisfy the desire.

Things went smoothly for quite a while. I would smoke marijuana and really get excited by the strange feeling it gave me. This didn't last, though. Before I knew it I was offered different types of pills including LSD. There was no question in my mind, I wanted to get higher so I took whatever came my way.

By the time I was 16 years old I was pushing marijuana. About three months after I started "dealing big," I was arrested. The charges were sales and possession of a dangerous drug. I was sentenced to five years' probation, but this didn't stop me. Right through high school I continued pushing drugs.

After I graduated from high school, I went on to college. After three months I dropped out. With no job to support the desire I had for drugs, I began to steal and cheat.

My life was completely hopeless. Then I found out about Teen Challenge and how God could make a new person out of me through Jesus Christ, His Son. It's been above five months since I entered the program and accepted Jesus Christ as my personal Savior. Since then I've had a joy in my heart that has carried me through five months with no desire to return to the old life of drugs. I now have a purpose in life. Jesus Christ created this change in me, and I want to serve Him in any way I can. There is no other person on earth or anywhere else that could change such a lost soul as mine into a new creature. Jesus Christ is the answer!

DAVID

I would like to start by telling you how I got involved with drugs. At the age of 13 I noticed that my brother was addicted to heroin. I saw all the suffering that my mother had to go through because of him. I said to myself that I would never take this drug. But as I grew older all my friends began to smoke pot. I didn't know what it was, but I remember that my friend Joe gave me some. I smoked it and felt good. Then I began to laugh at everything that I saw, because this was the effect of the pot.

I smoked pot for two years. It wasn't long before I was taking "goof balls" and hanging around the streets. It was here that I began getting into trouble. These "goof balls" had me bound for three years. My brother was still on heroin. I used to tell myself that I would never use heroin, but what I didn't realize was that my habit was getting bigger and the pills no longer could supply my need. I had to resort to heroin. While I was in prison my brother wrote to me about Teen Challenge.

He tried to explain to me the great change that had taken place in his life while he was at Teen Challenge. I was happy to receive his letter, even though I didn't believe him. At times I thought there might be hope because of what he had told me. But soon I was back out on the street strung out. I was sick, and I had taken an overdose several times. I went to Puerto Rico to try to escape the drug, but I didn't succeed. One day I remembered what my brother had told me about Teen Challenge. My mother had to put me out of our house. It was in desperate need that I went to Teen Challenge for the purpose of kicking my habit.

When I got there I saw all those ex-junkes praising God. I said to myself, "If God can help them, He can help me." I asked them if they would pray with me. It was here that I accepted the Lord into my heart by faith. I am now at the Training Center praising God for the work He is doing in my life.

Chapter 6

Does the End Really Justify the Means?

When it comes to our children we often think it is OK to lie, as long as we have their best interest in mind. After working with drug addicts and young people for so many years, we are sure that they want straight answers.

After a young man has been in our program long enough to get his health back, he usually thinks up some kind of reason to get a pass to see his family or friends. Our answer is always the same; we say "no." The reply is usually the same, "What's the matter, don't you trust me?" It's very easy to put yourself in a trap and say, "Yes, I trust you, but it would be better to stay here," or "We have a rule that there are no passes for the first three months." These answers lead to one big hassle. "Well, if you trust me, let me go, because I really need to see my family." "My problem is different; I must have a pass."

We have learned one very important lesson here. When we are faced with this type of situation we say, "No, I don't trust you. You have not been here long enough to have a pass, and we simply do not trust you." We also tell them they have not shown us anything to cause us to trust them. We have asked these boys months later what their feelings were about our not trusting them. They all were thankful that we were straight with them and they appreciated our sharing our true feelings of mistrust.

One of the boys I remember most is Joe M. After a few days at Teen Challenge, he asked if he could go home alone and see his mother for some money to buy clothes. We said, "No, we don't trust you. If we let you go you will get high." He gave us a look that would have killed us, if looks could kill. About one year after that he told us that if we had let him go, he would never have come back. He said he wanted to go home for only one reason— to get money from his mother, leaving her with the thought that he was going to get some needed clothing. As an addict he had sold or pawned everything he owned. Instead of getting clothes, however, he planned to go to a pusher for that bag of white powder and get high. He said, "If you would have done anything else except be honest with me, I would not have made it." Joe is a Bible school student today, which is amazing as he had been an addict for ten years.

After a high school assembly program once, we talked to a group of 10th graders. The subject of dating came up. We asked them what time they had to be home. Most of the answers were 10:30 and 11:30. No one said after midnight. We asked how many asked their parents for permission to stay out later. Most of them said they would like to stay out all night. Some said they asked their parents to allow them to stay out later, but they knew if they were allowed to they would only get into trouble of some sort.

If these kids knew the chances of getting into trouble after midnight (for example) were so great, why did they fight with their parents about the hour of coming home? We learned a valuable lesson we want you to take hold of: they were playing games with their parents. In the hassle with their parents, many would use the same argument some of our Teen Challenge fellows used, "What's the matter, don't you trust me?"

Now, Mom and Dad, are you going to shoot straight, or cop out? Many parents said, "Of course we trust you, *but*—" But what? Either you do, or you don't! The kids wanted their parents to say, "NO! I don't trust you." The kids knew that after midnight in most cities anything wholesome is closed. They knew that they were not mature enough to handle the situation. They just wanted to know if their parents were honest enough to express their feelings.

Parents, if you don't trust your children in certain cases, tell them. The truth may hurt, but they will respect you. If you lie, or try to con them they will put you in a category they already have most adults— hypo, or phony. Believe us, kids are sick and tired of phonies. They have a deep down respect for honest parents.

Chapter 7
Somebody,
Please Love Me!

One of the high points for many of the fellows at Teen Challenge Training Center is a visit from Rev. Lester Eisenburger, director of counseling at Teen Challenge. Rev. Eisenburger has deep insight into the many complex problems and hang-ups in which drug addicts can get involved. Along with this insight there is a pure heart of love for these fellows. He has also been able to use his many years of experience in psychology and therapy to help boys see hidden problems that they cannot understand or deal with by themselves.

Many of our fellows have been cast out by their families, and they consider Brother Eisenburger not only a counselor and friend, but a father who loves them. As Brother Eisenburger's car comes up our driveway, he is given an enthusiastic welcome as the fellows run to him and express their joy at seeing him again.

However, not everyone responds so exuberantly to Rev. Eisenburger's visits. For some time we noticed Tim would stand off to the side and glare at the scene, his face seethed in anger. (After being on the road with Tim for about two weeks and getting to know him, I learned that he had many mixed feelings about his parents.)

After several months of glaring at Rev. Eisenburger with open hostility, Tim asked, "May I have a talk with you?" "Of course, Tim, I'd be happy to," he answered. After his first meeting with Rev. Eisenburger, Tim could understand why the guys loved him so much. His patience, love and understanding as he listened to Tim soon won his confidence. At the end of their first session together, Brother Eisenburger prayed with Tim, as he did with all the fellows who came to him.

During the first interview Tim told Rev. Eisenburger, "It makes me very angry to see so many fellows run and embrace you!" The reason was obvious—he was just plain jealous. Tim, too, wanted to hug him and be hugged in return. "In all my life I've never known what it means to be loved," Tim continued. Although Tim came from a good home where both parents had jobs in the five-figured column, he had never felt his parents' arms around him, nor heard them say, "Tim, I love you!" This left him with deep scars. He felt unloved, rejected, as though no one cared. The world seemed like a materialized merry-go-round. Therefore, when drugs appeared in his town, he went for them. Drugs offered him good feelings. They offered him a new culture, friends with the same kind of rejected feeling that he had. He took LSD over one hundred times.

He left home and went to live in Haight-Ashbury in San Francisco with his new culture. Here he said he felt "loved and accepted." He lived in a small apartment with ten kids who shared with each other all they had—drugs, food, clothes, love, sex, and money. Every one had run away from home, not because they were rebels against the Establishment or to dodge the army, but because they all felt that their parents did not care. They felt rejected and unwanted. All they saw was man working hard all day to get ahead, and the kids coming home to an empty house each night. Dad would work overtime, and when he didn't, it was always, "Sorry, this is my bowling night," or a "lodge night." No wonder the kids turned to drugs and the drug sub-culture, for there they felt loved.

However, it did not take long for them to see the farce in drugs. One by one the kids were disappearing. Some went to jail, others to different drug programs, but most of them went to mental wards in hospitals. Many of Tim's friends just freaked out. Everything was distorted. Nothing made sense to them anymore.

Tim heard about Teen Challenge while he was high on a trip. A minister, driving down the highway, stopped and picked up Tim and told him that God loved him and that Teen Challenge would offer the help, food, and housing that he needed. Right there Tim accepted the Lord, went to Teen Challenge and is now witnessing to others.

Almost every fellow we have talked to

who has been in the program has felt that his parents did not have a real love for him.

At the close of one of our PTA meetings we attended, Andy Busti, one of the fellows who came through the Teen Challenge program and stayed to work on the staff, stopped and looked very intently at the parents and some of the kids that were present, and said, "You parents complain about our rebellious youth, but when is the last time you walked up to your child and put your arms around him or her and said, 'Honey, I love you,' and just held him close? How about it, Mom and Dad, when was the last time?"

The heart-cry of thousands of kids like Tim is, "Somebody, please love me!"

Chapter 8

I Don't Want a Money Machine

At the close of a Civics Club meeting a very handsome, sharply dressed middle-aged man walked over to us and said, "*My son is a drug addict!* I gave him everything. He would come to me and ask for money to take out his girl, and I would give him fifty bucks. When he turned 16 I gave him a new $4,000 car. Where did I go wrong?"

Then one of our fellows said to him, "Your son did not want $50 per date and a new car. He wanted a father!" If I heard that once, I have heard it a thousand times.

Young men or women tell us that they have had very special problems. So they would go to their mother or dad and tell them that they had to talk to them, but the only response they would get from their parents would be a five or a ten dollar bill, or, "Tomorrow, I am busy now."

Being a parent today is one of the most serious considerations in life. Just what does it mean to be a parent? It means much more than bringing life into the world. Consider the following points.

1. Being a parent means more than of-

fering material things. Many parents feel that, because they either went through the depression or had it tough, they are not going to let that happen to their kids. So they offer money and more money. KIDS DON'T WANT THAT! They want a mother and dad who are involved with *them*.

2. Being a parent means *total* involvement. We must get involved in our kids' problems. We have to be involved today when they need us, not tomorrow. Saying I will listen tomorrow only puts up barriers. If we are going to be an effective involved parent, it may mean getting out of bed at 3 a.m. to listen to a problem. It may even mean listening when we are sick or tired, or sick and tired.

How does this chapter relate to drug education? When you offer money instead of yourself, or when you say, "Not today. I'm too tired," remember this: Drugs offer freedom from problems *now*. Such relief is temporary, but then drugs are easily obtained by the neglected youth.

Having the feeling that nobody cares is common among many of our young people. "If nobody cares, O.K., I will cop out and get high." You may think that this sounds a bit farfetched. But, after talking to thousands of kids on drugs and family problems, it is not in the least bit extreme. Many kids think this way.

Chapter 9

Scare The Hell Out Of Them!

Our phone rang quite early one morning. On the other end was a very frantic high school principal who had just realized that the problem of drug abuse was getting out of hand in his school. He said he had heard that Teen Challenge Training Center did high school prevention programs with a great deal of success, and he wondered if he could book our group. We set up the meeting, and just before we hung up the phone he said, "Come and do your program, but by all means *scare the hell out of them!*"

This tactic does not work! When the drug problem was first making the headlines, none of the most prevalent ways of dealing with the problem was scare tactics. It worked on some, but many more did not believe what they heard. They then tried drugs for themselves, and in doing so they discovered many falsehoods, such as:

1. *Anyone who smokes pot will go on to heroin addiction.*

Many parents have tried to trick their children into thinking that by smoking marijuana they would become a hard-core junkie in a short time. Kids, being as curious as they are today, have tried marijuana, liked it, and they did not turn into hard-core junkies right away. Because they liked the feeling and did not become hard-core addicts, they've discounted all that is being said about drug education, especially scare tactics.

2. Telling young innocent children that people who will try to hook them on drugs will be found lurking around school yards, bowling alleys, and candy stores, etc., is no longer valid. The simple fact is that it is usually your closest friend who will first introduce you to drugs.

3. The statements that all addicts look dirty and grimy, their behavior is very bazaar, and that they act like low, dirty animals, are not true. The truth is that most addicts are neat and clean, and they present themselves very well. It is hard to pick them out; one almost has to have medical tests to prove addiction of any kind.

4. The statement that all drug abusers are bent on committing murder, rape, and other crimes of violence while they are high is also untrue. They want to be left alone; they want to be quiet where they can just be high. When a drug addict is sick and in need of money in order to get another fix, he may then become very violent or capable of murder if stopped in some way from getting his source of life.

It is true that illegal possession of pot and pills carries heavy penalties, but hardly anyone arrested in their teen years does any real jail time for drugs. Most teenagers know that they will get off with probation or nothing at all. Teenagers have the right to a lawyer, and if they get one, the chances are they will get off. One of the fellows at Teen Challenge was arrested eleven times for different crimes, including possession of drugs. He never did any time because he had enough money to get a good lawyer. As a result of this, he is not afraid of the law. The judicial system means very little to most young people.

One of the most frequent questions we are asked is, "What do you tell an addict, and how do you convince him to come into Teen Challenge?" After talking to thousands of addicts, we conclude that most drug addicts know they are in bad shape, and they are looking for something to get them out of the mess they are in. We have simply shared with them that Christ has a way out for them. It is not only a way out, but also a way of life that is beautiful. Even though we believe in the doctrine of heaven and hell, it would be tragic to walk up to a drug addict and say, "Look, buddy, you are a degenerate, and you are going to hell when you die." I think a great majority would look at us and reply, "I am in hell now. How can it get worse?"

Scare tactics do not work with our youth. If we are going to save them from drug addiction, or just save them from a dull, boring existence, we must offer them something dynamic, exciting, and powerful, something worth living and dying for. This something is the fullness of Jesus Christ.

Chapter 10

How To Raise a Potential Drug Addict

Live by the following rules very carefully, and the possibility of your children becoming involved with drugs or lawlessness is almost certain.

1. From the time of their birth give your children everything they want. Never say "no." You would not want to hurt their mental growth.

2. When your children use foul words, laugh at them and say it is "cute." This will encourage him to pick up certain phrases that will blow the top off your head later.

3. Never teach anything from the Bible. Offer no spiritual help. Let the children wait until they are 21; then they can decide for themselves.

4. Never admit you are wrong. Never teach your children to say they are sorry or admit that they are wrong. If you or your child admit that you are wrong, it could cause a guilt complex. Later, if your child is ever arrested for any reason, he will feel that society is against him and he is being persecuted.

5. Let them throw all responsibility on

others. Never let them accept responsibility. Pick up for them. Do everything for them.

6. Let them read anything they want to read.

7. Fight openly in front of the family. If the home is broken up, the children will not be shocked by doing so.

8. You had it tough as a kid; so give your kids all the money that they need. Do not let them have hard times like you had.

9. Satisfy their every craving for food, drink, and comfort. See that every sensual desire is satisfied. Denial may lead to harmful frustration.

10. If they ever get into real trouble, defend yourself by saying, "That little brat. I never could do anything with him!"

11. Take their part against peers, neighbors, teachers, and policemen.

12. Drink and smoke in front of your kids, but be sure to tell them about the harmful effects of drugs.

13. Never take your kids to the museum, bowling, fishing, etc., for fun. Believe that you and your children are in two different worlds. You live in yours, and your children live in theirs.

14. Believe in the motto, "Do as I say, not as I do."

Now, parents, follow these rules and prepare for a life of grief, because it is coming. Or, try, with God's help, to set an example. Your authority will be challenged again and again. Your motives will be questioned. Try the honest approach and start NOW!

Chapter 11

One Way—What Does It Mean?

In the last few years, you have probably seen one or two or even a group of young people pass each other on the street. When they did, you saw two fingers go heavenward. You may have said to yourself, "What is that all about?" It just means victory or peace. Now, just when you are getting used to those two fingers, something new has happened. Some young people are now sticking only one finger in the air as they greet one another.

What is that all about? It's the new Jesus Movement. The young people are signaling each other that there is only one way to find peace, joy, love, forgiveness, and satisfaction. Only one way to find release from personal problems such as booze, drugs, and deviate sexual acts.

This move to God is one of the greatest things that has happened in years! From coast to coast, thousands and thousands of young people are looking to God or the *One Way* to real life. The Bible has quite a few interesting things to say about the One Way.

In John 14:6, Jesus says, "I am the

WAY, I am the truth, I am the life. NO man can go to the Father except by me." In Acts 4:12, the Bible says, "Salvation is to be found through Him alone; for there is no one else in all the world, whose name God has given to men, by whom we can be saved." The Bible also states in Proverbs 14:12: "There is a WAY that seems right to men, but the end thereof are the ways of death." There are many more verses in the Bible that show us there is only *ONE WAY* to find real life!

When you see a young person with one finger pointed heavenward, that's good! Don't worry about that type of a young person. They're going the right WAY.

We are running into some weird things in schools from the fad "Jesus freak" and the zealous without knowledge. Therefore there is a need for guidance and Bible teaching. We need to encourage these young people. They may not be too orthodox and they may upset the "normal" routine of our churches. Let us do our part to get them grounded in God's Word so that the experience they have found can grow into a beautiful life. Paul exhorted us to "grow in the grace and knowledge of our Lord and Saviour Jesus Christ."

Chapter 12

Get Your Home Together

God has a definite order for our households. If we put our house in proper order, many problems and frustrations which frequently occur in bringing up a family will work themselves out and, in many cases, disappear.

The following is God's order for our homes: First of all, Christ must be the Lord and Master of the entire home. We must start here to make it as a family.

Second, husbands must be the head of the home, and they are directly responsible to Christ for their families. Shortly after I was married, I handed a pair of trousers to my new wife and told her to put them on. She gave me an odd look and said, "They're too big!" I replied, "Please remember that!" Then I quoted the Bible verse that says wives are to be in submission to their own husbands. She said she planned to be in submission, but reminded me that the Bible also says I must love her just as Christ loved and gave Himself for the church.

Many husbands stop with the verse on submission. Husbands sometimes need to be reminded that they must love their wives just as Christ loved the church.

Third, wives are to be a help meet to their husbands, and the head of the house in the husband's absence.

Fourth, the children are to obey their parents. Many people believe they should let their children express themselves in any way. I have talked with a great number of ex-drug addicts, and by their own admission permissiveness is a direct link to drug addiction.

A positive home life must be established. A better way, a way that provides true peace and happiness. Chapter 11 outlines the plan of personal salvation through Jesus Christ. But that experience must be added to. It will take the total effort and dedication of the entire family to create the strong family unit that can stand the onslaught of this present world.

You may read this and feel "we have messed it up." Start *now!* You cannot undo the past, but you can do something about the future. Here is the story of how Demi and Cookie got it together.

LOOK WHAT GOD HAS PUT TOGETHER

Because I (Cookie) was raised in a very poor home, from the time I was a very little girl my only thought was of ways to make a quick buck. I found a way at age 14 while attending junior high school. I began selling pot on the playground. This did not last long, because I got busted. I went to court and was put in a home for delinquent girls for a 90-day sentence. A year and a half later I was home. That year and a half was the longest "90 days" I ever lived. I was so lonely I just ached, but I covered it up by causing all sorts of trouble. Consequently, my sentence stretched out for another 450 days.

I was out of jail for only two weeks when I found myself injecting heroin into my veins. In a very short time I was a hard-knock junkie. I acted hard and bitter, but I wanted a clean life more than anything else.

For about five years I was in almost every kind of program New York had. They ranged from a 21-day methadone cure to a private therapy program.

A Christian who went to John 3:16 Church in the Bronx told me about the love of God. He also told me about Teen Challenge. I just simply sniffed around Teen Challenge.

At age 23 I was really bad off. I had just been released from court. I had come out of a situation that had caved in half my face. I was getting high on both goof balls and heroin. I walked into Teen Challenge high on both. They explained to me I would have to come back the next day; they had no empty beds. Rev. Ruth Cowgill told Don Wilkerson she would take me to her apartment and give up her own bed. This kind of love almost knocked me dead. I responded to God's love and completed the program. Also I attended Bible School for one year. During the summer I met Demi and fell in love with him. (Demi, like Cookie, was a drug addict for many years.)

Demi says:

Early in my teens my cousin told me about a bag of white powder that would turn me on. It did. It took me only three weeks to get hooked, but it took about 15 years to turn off. It was not long till I wanted out, so I enrolled in a city program. After I had completed the course I received a piece of paper that said I was clean. But with that piece of paper in my pocket I got high again. For years my life was spent in and out of jails and programs. Then my dad took me in his taxi-cab to a large Federal hospital in Kentucky. I was there only a short time. Part of their treatment was a pill that was to make one forget heroin. Under the influence of this pill, I saw visions, colored creeping things, animals of all sizes, cyclops, fish, things that creep, crawl and fly. I did not forget about heroin; instead, I wanted more.

The day came that I was to go home. They told me the best way to be clean was to let a truck run me down and kill me. I did not let a truck hit me, so it was not long before I was hooked and back in Kentucky. This time I knew I would die a junkie, so I tried to kill myself. I wasn't successful here either. I had heard about Teen Challenge, so when I left the hospital I went straight to the Center. They told me I was a sinner, and drugs was one of the forms of sin I had chosen. God forgave me of this sin and dried up my desire to get high.

After a few weeks I went back to the Teen Challenge Training Center. For several months this is where I learned of the deep love of God. These months at the Training Center were when I really got myself together. From the Training Center I went to Bible School. During my summer vacation Cookie not only fell in love with me, but I fell in love with her as well. We believe God wanted us together, so we were married. We moved to Columbus, Ohio, and learned to live together as a Christian family. After a while God showed us that He had more in mind for us. We felt we should go back to New York and work in the great cement jungle. We were rescued out of this jungle, and God has us back in the middle of it. We are a testimony of God's wonderful grace. Our desire is to let as many drug addicts as possible see the salvation of our God.

(Editor's note: Demi and Cookie have been faithfully serving God for over six years.)

Drug Glossary

Acapulco gold—A very high grade of marijuana.

Acid—LSD, LSD-25 (lysergic acid diethylamide).

Acidhead—Frequent user of LSD.

Acid test—A term coined by the Kesey group to label a rock and roll dance performed to multiple sound and light effects.

Back track—Withdraw the plunger of a syringe before injecting drugs to make sure needle is in the right place.

Bag—Packet of drugs.

Ball—Absorption of stimulants and cocaine via genitalia

Balloon—Rubber toy balloon used for storing or delivering heroin.

Bang—Injection of drugs.

Barbs—Barbiturates.

Bennies—Benzedrine, an amphetamine.

Bindle—Packet of narcotics.

Blank—Extremely low-grade narcotics.

Blast—Strong effect from a drug.

Blow a stick—To smoke marijuana.

Blue angels—Amytal, a barbiturate.

Blue heaven—Amytal.

Blue velvet—Paregoric (camphorated tincture of opium) and pyribenzamine (an antihistamine) mixed and injected.

Bombita—Amphetamine injection, sometimes taken with heroin.

Bread—Money.

Bum trip—Bad experience with psychedelics.

Bummer—Bad experience with psychedelics.

Busted—Arrested.

Buttons—The sections of the peyote cactus.

Can—One ounce of marijuana. Term derived from tobacco can in which marijuana was commonly sold in the past. Now more frequently observed in small paper bags.

Cap—A capsule of heroin.

Chipping—Taking narcotics occasionally.

Clean—Free from narcotics.

Coasting—Under the influence of drugs.

Cocktail—Attaching marijuana butt to a regular tobacco cigarette.

Cokie—Cocaine addict.

Cold turkey—Sudden withdrawal of narcotics (from the gooseflesh, which resembles the skin of a cold plucked turkey).

Coming down—Coming off the high one gets from drugs.

Connection—Drug supplier.

Cook—An underground chemist who manufactures and sells illegal speed, LSD and heroin, etc.

Cop—To obtain heroin

Cop out—Quit, take off, confess, defect, inform.

Crash—The effects of stopping the use of amphetamines.

Crash pad—Place where the user withdraws from amphetamines.

Crutch—Device used to hold marijuana cigarette when it has burned to the point where it will burn your fingers.

Cubehead—Frequent user of LSD.

Cut—Dilute drugs by adding milk, sugar or another inert substance.

Dealer—Drug supplier.

Deck—Packet of narcotics.

Dexies—Dexedrine, an amphetamine.

Dime bag—$10 package of narcotics.

Dirty—Possessing drugs, liable to arrest if searched.

DMT—(Dimethyltryptamine). A short-acting psychedelic drug that is injected or smoked.

Dollies—Dolophine (also known as methadone), a synthetic narcotic.

Dope—Narcotic.

Doper—Person who uses drugs regularly.

Downers—Sedatives, alcohol, tranquilizers, and narcotics.

Drop—Swallow a drug.

Dummy—Purchase which did not contain narcotics.

Dynamite—High-grade heroin.

Fix—Injection of narcotics.

Flash—The initial feeling after injection.

Flip—Become psychotic.

Floating—Under the influence of drugs.

Freakout—Bad experience with psychedelics; also a chemical high.

Fuzz—The police.

Gage—Marijuana.

Garbage—Inferior heroin (diluted).

Geeze—Injection of narcotic.

Good trip—Happy experience with psychedelics.

Goofball—Barbiturate combined with an amphetamine, or an upper and a downer taken together.

Goofing—Under the influence of drugs effecting a drunken-like manner.

Grateful dead, the—A West Coast rock and roll group under entrepreneural aegis of Owsley Stanley.

Great white light—Relating to the aspects of transcendental experiences during one stage of which conceptual vision may be seen as all-encompassing white light.

Guide—A person who baby sits for the psychedelic user during a session.

Guru—A person who acts as one's teacher and guide.

Grass—Marijuana.

H—Heroin.

Habit—Addiction to drugs.

Hard narcotics—Opiates, such as heroin, morphine.

Hard stuff—Morphine, cocaine, heroin.

Hash—Hashish, the resin of Cannabis.

Hay—Marijuana.

Head—Person dependent on drugs.

Hearts—Dexedrine tablets (from the shape).

Heat—The police.

High—Under the influence of drugs.

Holding—Having drugs in one's possession.

Hog—An addict who takes all the drugs he can get his hands on.

Hooked—Addicted.

Hophead—Narcotics addict.

Horse—Heroin.

Hustle—Activities involved in obtaining money to buy heroin.

Hustler—Prostitute.

Hype—Narcotics addict.

Ice cream habit—Small habit of drugs.

Joint—Marijuana cigarette.

Jolly beans—Pep pills.

Joy-pop—Inject narcotics irregularly.

Junkie—Narcotics addict.

Karma—Fate. The force generated by a person's actions that is held in Hinduism and Buddhism to be the motive power for the round of rebirths and deaths endured by him until he has achieved spiritual liberation and freed himself from the effects of such force.

Kee—Kilo 2.2 pounds.

Kick the habit—Stop using narcotics (from the withdrawal leg muscle twitches).

Layout—Equipment for injecting drug.

Lemonade—Poor heroin.

Loaded—High on drugs.

LSD—Lysergic acid diethylamide tartrate.

M—Morphine.

Mainline—Inject drugs into a vein.

Maintaining—Keeping at a certain level of drug effect.

Make a buy—To buy drugs.

Man, the—The police.

Mandala—A graphic mystic symbol of the universe that is typically in the form of a circle enclosing a square and often bearing symmetrically arranged representations of deities. It is used chiefly in Hinduism and Buddhism as an aid to meditation.

Manicure—Remove the dirt, seeds, and stem from marijuana.

Mary Jane—Marijuana.

Maya—The powerful force that creates the cosmic illusion that the phenomenal world is real.

MCG—Microgram. A thousandth of a milligram.

Mesc—Mescaline, the alkaloid in peyote.

Meth—Methamphetamine.

Methhead—Habitual user of methamphetamine.

MG—Milligram. A thousandth of a gram.

Mikes—Micrograms (millionths of a gram).

Monkey—A drug habit.

Narc—Narcotics detective.

Nickel bag—$5 packet of drugs.

O.D.—Overdose of narcotics.

On a trip—Under the influence of LSD or other hallucinogens.

On the nod—Sleepy from narcotics.

Opiate—A class of drugs which have the properties and action of opium. Includes opium itself and derivatives of opium as well as synthetic opiate-like drugs not derived from opium.

Outfit—Equipment for injection by the hypodermic route. It includes cotton, eyedropper, needle, spoon and a belt.

Panic—Shortage of narcotics on the market.

Pig—Derogatory for police officer.

Pillhead—Heavy user of pills, barbiturates or amphetamines or both.

Pop—Inject drugs.

Pot—Marijuana.

Pothead—Heavy marijuana user.

Psychedelic—Mind manifesting.

Purple hearts—Dexamyl, a combination of dexedrine and amytal (from the shape and color).

Pusher—Drug peddler.

Quill—A matchbook cover for sniffing methedrine, cocaine, or heroin.

Rainbows—Tuinal (amytal and seconal), a barbiturate combination in a blue and red capsule.

Red devils—Seconal, a barbiturate.

Reefer—Marijuana cigarette.

Reentry—Return from a trip.

Roach—Marijuana butt.

Roach holder—Device for holding the butt of a marijuana cigarette.

Run—An amphetamine binge.

Satch cotton—Cotton used to strain drugs before injection; may be used again if supplies are gone.

Satori—A sudden enlightenment and a state of consciousness attained by intuitive illlumination representing the spiritual goal of Zen Buddhism.

Scag—Heroin.

Score—Make a purchase of drugs.

Shooting gallery—Place where addicts inject.

Short—A car.

Skin popping—Injecting drugs under the skin.

Smack—Heroin.

Smoke—Wood alcohol.

Sniffing—Taking drugs through the nose.

Snorting—Inhaling drugs.

Snow—Cocaine.

Speed—Methamphetamine.

Speedball—A powerful shot of drug. Usually heroin or morphine and cocaine combined.

Speedfreak—Habitual user of speed.

Split—Run away.

Stash—Supply of drugs in a secure place.

Stick—Marijuana cigarette.

Stoned—Denoting other than normal consciousness, induced by chemicals or use of alcohol.

Stoolie—Informer.

Straight—A person who does not take drugs.

Strung out—Addicted.

Taste—A sample of drugs.

Tea—Marijuana.

Toke up—To light a marijuana cigarette.

Tolerance—An adaptive state characterized by diminished response to the same quantity of drug or by the fact that a larger dose is required to produce the same degree of pharmac-dynamic effect.

Tracks—Scars along veins after many injections.

Travel agent—In the context of psychedelic use the person who provides the trip.

Tripping out—High on psychedelics.

Turned on—Under the influence of drugs.

Turps—Elixir of Terpin Hydrate with Codeine, a cough syrup.

Uppers—Stimulants, cocaine, and psychedelics.

Users—One who uses narcotics.

Vodka acid—Vodka that contains LSD, considered by many to be the most readily available preservative for the chemical.

Weed—Marijuana.

Weed head—Marijuana smoker.

Wheels—Auto.

Whites—Amphetamine.

White stuff—Morphine.

Works—Equipment for injecting drugs.

Yellow jacket—Nembutal, a barbiturate.

Yen sleep—A drowsy, restless state during the withdrawal period.

Zig zag—Paper used to roll marijuana cigarettes.